SNOWBOARDING

Frances Ridley

Editorial Consultant – Cliff Moon

visit

JN 04180352

nasen
Helping Everyone Achieve

nasen
NASEN House, 4/5 Amber Business Village, Amber Close, Amington, Tamworth, Staffordshire B77 4RP

Rising Stars UK Ltd.
22 Grafton Street, London W1S 4EX
www.risingstars-uk.com

Every effort has been made to trace copyright holders and obtain their permission for use of copyright material. The publisher will gladly receive information enabling them to rectify any error or omission in subsequent editions.

All facts are correct at time of going to press.

Published 2006

Cover design: Button plc
Cover image: Thinkstock/Alamy
Illustrator: Bill Greenhead
Technical artwork: IFA Design
Text design and typesetting: Nicholas Garner, Codesign
Technical advisers: Martin Lazell and Tom Cloke
Educational consultants: Cliff Moon and Lorraine Petersen
Pictures: Snow-Camp: page 12. Alamy: pages 5, 13, 15, 18, 19, 21, 22, 23, 38, 39. Buzz Pictures: pages 4, 5, 6, 7, 9, 10, 11, 12, 20, 22, 26, 28, 29, 34, 36, 37, 38, 39, 40, 41, 42. Getty Images: page 43.

British Library Cataloguing in Publication Data.
A CIP record for this book is available from the British Library.

ISBN: 1-905056-92-3

Printed by Craft Print International Ltd, Singapore

This book should not be used as a guide to the sports shown in it. The publishers accept no responsibility for any harm which might result from taking part in these sports.

Contents

What is snowboarding?

Snowboarding is a **board sport**.

Snowboarders use their boards to ride down the mountain slopes.

They also do tricks on their boards.

Snowboarding started in the 1960s.

At first, only a few people went snowboarding.

Then, more and more people got into it.

Now, you can go snowboarding at most **ski resorts**.

Snow Fact!

The James Bond film, *A View to a Kill*, helped make snowboarding popular.

Three ways to snowboard

There are three ways to snowboard.

Kit

Soft boots

Mid-length board

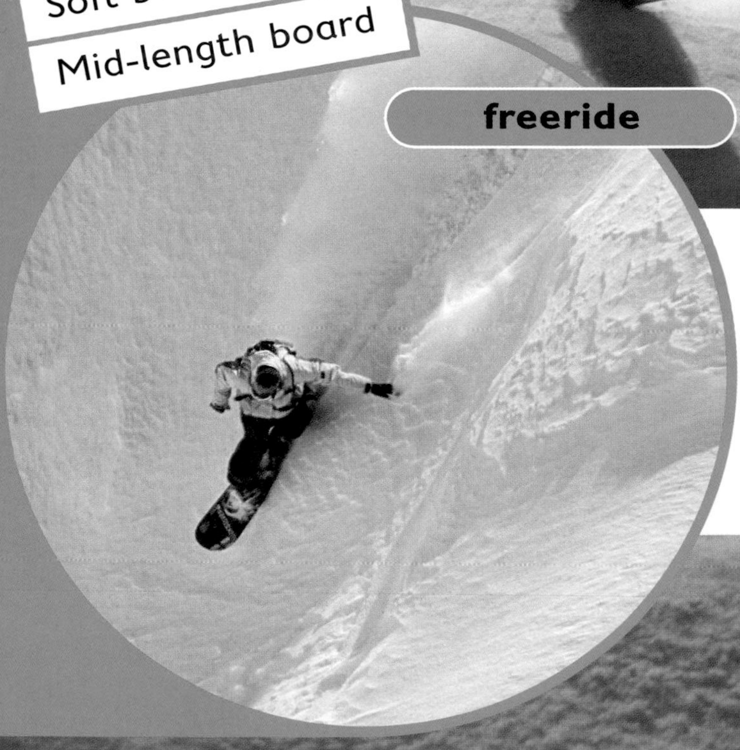

freeride

You can ride on a snowboard.

This is called freeride snowboarding.

You can do tricks on a snowboard.

This is called freestyle snowboarding.

freestyle

Kit

Soft boots

Short board

freecarve

You can race on a snowboard.

This is called freecarve snowboarding.

Kit

Hard boots

Long board

Snowboards

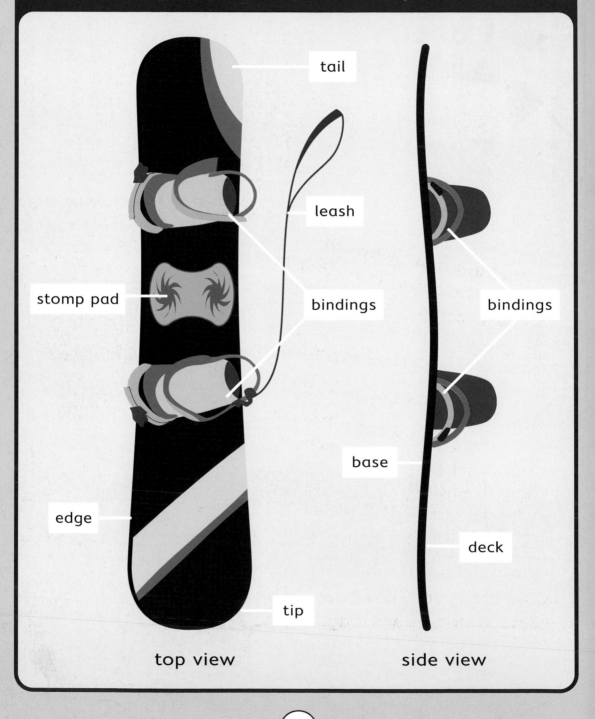

tail

leash

stomp pad

bindings

bindings

base

edge

deck

tip

top view

side view

But there are lots of different snowboards.

Tips!

Picking a snowboard
Pick the snowboard that is best for you. Think about these things:

- How heavy are you?
- How big are your feet?
- Do you want a freeride, freestyle or freecarve board?

Look after your snowboard – keep it in a **board bag**.

Snowboarding kit

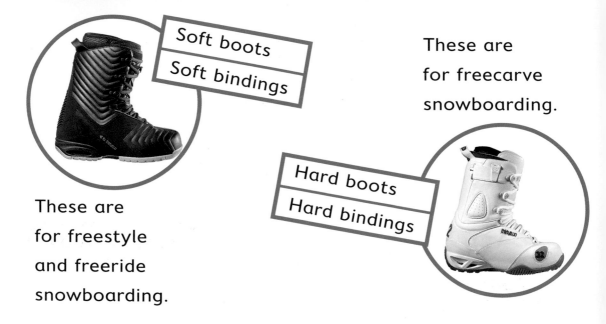

Soft boots
Soft bindings

These are for freecarve snowboarding.

Hard boots
Hard bindings

These are for freestyle and freeride snowboarding.

Warm clothes

Wear three layers of clothes to keep warm.
You also need gloves and a hat.

The bottom layer keeps heat next to your body.

The middle layer keeps you warm and dry.

The top layer keeps the rain and wind off.

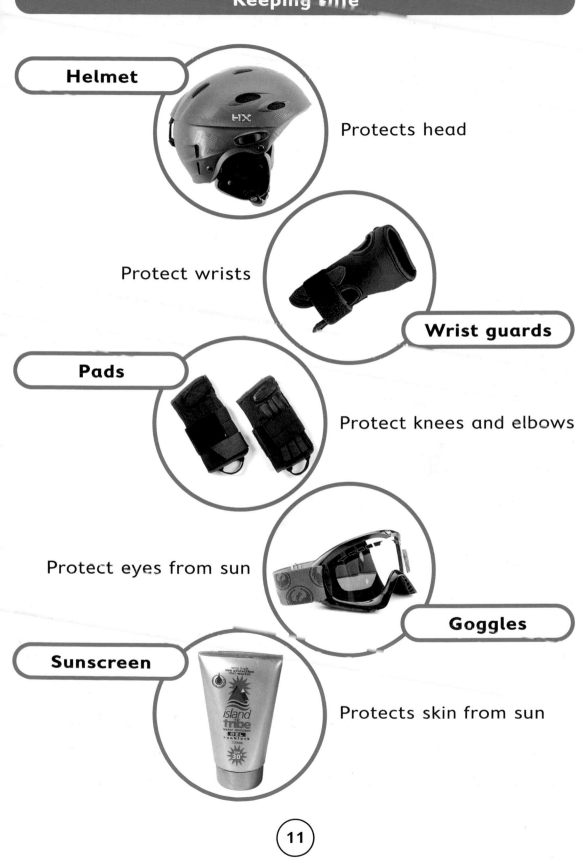

Helmet

Protects head

Protect wrists

Wrist guards

Pads

Protect knees and elbows

Protect eyes from sun

Goggles

Sunscreen

Protects skin from sun

Get into snowboarding

A holiday is a good way to start snowboarding.

Most **ski resorts** do snowboarding.

You get lessons and you can borrow a snowboard and kit.

Snow-Camp is a winter sports charity.

It takes kids on snowboarding holidays.

Some schools do snowboarding trips.

Lots of snowboarders go to Tignes in France.

Where to go

Country	Snow	Snowboard rating	Cost
USA	All year round	*****	Costs more than France and Scotland
France	Only in winter	***	Costs more than Scotland Costs less than USA
Scotland	Only in winter	**	Costs less than USA and France

Snowboarding in the UK

You don't have to go on holiday to snowboard.

I have not been on holiday yet.

I want to learn snowboarding before I go.

I went on holiday last year.

I want to get better at snowboarding.

I'm not going on holiday.

I just love snowboarding!

At real snow centres the snow is made by machine.

A **snow cannon** making snow

Dry-ski slopes are outdoors. The 'snow' is a plastic sheet. It is smooth but not hard.

Shredders (Part one)

Jez was good-looking and rich. He was top at *everything* and Kim was his girl.

Tom was not good-looking or rich. He wasn't top at anything and he wished that Kim was *his* girl.

It was the first morning of the snowboarding trip. Everybody was going to the hire shop. Jez had his own boots and snowboard, so he stayed in bed.

Jez was late for the lesson.

Eddie was the instructor. He was cross with Jez.

"You have hard boots and a freestyle board," he shouted. "Go to the hire shop – now!"

Jez missed the first lesson.

"So what?" Jez said. "I don't need lessons, anyway."

But Jez *did* need lessons.

He was top at everything at school – but he was rubbish at snowboarding.

Continued on page 24

Snowboard basics

1. Warm up your body before you start.

Snowboarders doing a warm-up

Look at the snowboarder in this picture.
She has her left foot in front.
She is **regular**.

Some riders have their right foot in front.
They are **goofy**.

Head up

Knees bent

Feet in bindings

Regular or goofy?

1 Slide across a shiny floor with your socks on.

2 Check which foot goes in front.

3 Put this foot in front on your snowboard.

The bottom of the bunny slope

The **bunny slope** is not very steep.
It is a good place to start snowboarding.
Start at the bottom of the slope.

Moving along

Learn to **skate** and **glide**.

Tip!

Don't strap your back foot into the bindings.

Stopping and turning

Learn to use the edges of your board. They help you stop and turn.

Tip!

The edges of your board are called heelside and toeside.

Now, take the chairlift to the top of the **bunny slope**.

Tip!

Chairlifts don't stop moving – get in and out as fast as you can!

Moving along

Learn how to **glide** across the slope.

Learn how to turn your board.

Warning! Strap both your feet into the bindings!

Moving like this is called the 'falling leaf'.

You use your heelside edge to glide across the slope and back again.

Setting your speed

Learn how to set your speed.

Make your board go slower or faster.

Warning! Keep your downhill edge out of the snow or you will fall over.

Tips!

Everyone falls over when they start to snowboard.

- Wear wrist guards.
- Don't fall on you hands – fall on your elbows.

Shredders (Part two)

Tom loved snowboarding. He was good at it!

The other kids asked him how to do things. He liked showing them – but he never showed off.

Jez made jokes about Kim when she fell over. Soon, Kim was sick of it.

She spent more and more time with Tom.

On Thursday, they got a chairlift to the top of the slope.

"It's my last day," said Tom to himself. "I have to make the most of it."

"Go for it!" said Eddie. "Remember everything I've told you."

Kim went first. She was good. Tom felt proud of her.

Jez went next He was going too fast.

Then it was Tom's turn ...

Continued on page 30

Freeride

Lots of people do freeride snowboarding.

You can ride and jump.

You can go all over the mountain.

A freeride board

They have a long nose.

They are mid-length and narrow.

Tip!

Wear soft boots and bindings with a freeride board.

Freeriders like to ride on powder snow.

Powder snow is snow that has just fallen. Nobody else has been on it yet.

Out in the mountains

The best powder snow isn't in the **ski resorts**, it's in the mountains.

Riding in the mountains is hard. You have to be good at snowboarding.

You have to ride on hard ice and powder snow, and around trees and rocks.

Backpack

Safety tips

X Don't ride in the mountains on your own.

✓ Do tell people where you are going.

Take a backpack when you freeride in the mountains. Pack these things in it.

Don't forget:
Food and hot drink
First-aid kit
Avalanche kit

repair kits

screwdriver

avalanche shovel

avalanche probe

collapsible poles

snowshoes

knife

Shredders (Part three)

Tom was nearly at the bottom.
Suddenly, Jez fell.

Jez didn't remember what Eddie had told them.
He fell on to his hands.

Tom went over to Jez. Eddie was close behind.

"I've hurt my wrists," said Jez. He was crying
with pain.

"Tom, take Jez back," said Eddie. "I'll tell the
doctor to meet you."

Tom and Jez went to the hotel.

"I bet you're loving this," said Jez. "I bet you're going to tell everybody."

Tom didn't say anything. He felt sorry for Jez, but he felt sorry for himself, too. He was missing the last lesson.

The doctor came. He told Tom to go back to the others.

But the lesson was over.

Continued on the next page

That evening, Eddie gave out prizes.

"The prize for the best snowboarder goes to …"

Tom held his breath. Was he the best snowboarder?

"… Dan King," said Eddie.

Everybody cheered. Dan was very good, but he'd been snowboarding before.

"The next prize is for the best team player," said Eddie. "For having a go – and getting on with everybody. It goes to Tom Selby."

Everybody cheered again.

"You wanted the other prize, didn't you?" said Eddie.

"Yes," said Tom. "But this is good."

"It's a free visit to the snow centre," said Eddie. "Keep up the good work, Tom!"

The disco started. Kim came over. She looked great.

"Do you want to dance?" she asked.

"Do you need to ask?" said Tom.

Freestyle

Freestyle riding is good fun.

You do tricks in the air and on the ground.

You jump and spin.

The boards are not heavy. They are short and fat with **twin-tips**.

Freestyle boards let you do lots of things.

Tip!

Wear soft boots and bindings with a freestyle board.

Snowboard films

Snowboard films show a lot of freestyle tricks.

Snowboarding professionals show off their skills and the tricks look good on film.

Snowboard parks

You can do freestyle tricks in a snowboard park.

Snowboard parks have half-pipes, jumps and rails.

A half-pipe is a U-shape cut
into the snow.
You ride up and down the U.

There are lots of
kinds of jump.
This is a tabletop
jump.

A rail is a
metal bar.
You slide down it.

Freestyle tricks

There are lots of tricks. Here are some of them.

The ollie

You do this trick on the ground.

You jump into the air with the board.

You do this trick in the half-pipe.

You spin round in the air with the board.

Alley-oop

Fakie to forward

You do this trick on a slope.

You turn round on the board as you go downhill.

You do this trick off a jump.

You flip off the jump backwards.

Back flip

Freecarve

Freecarving is when you race on your snowboard.

Freecarve **runs** have lots of corners.

You have to turn the corners very fast.

Fact!
Freecarving is sometimes called alpine snowboarding.

Freecarve boards are long, thin and stiff.

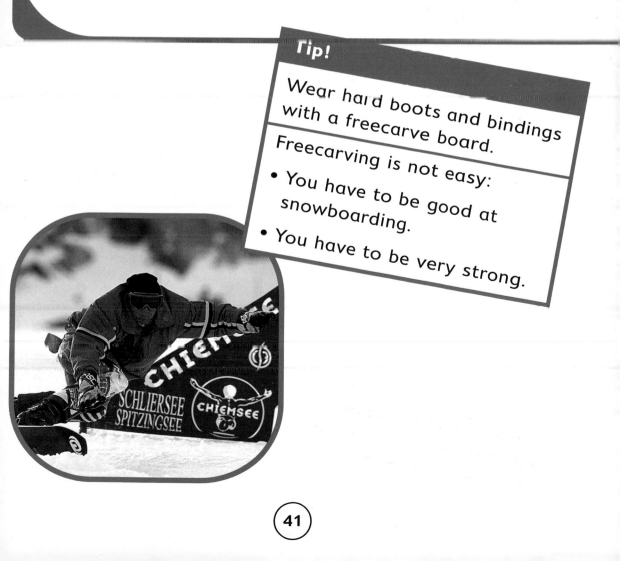

They go fast and they are good at corners.

Tip!

Wear hard boots and bindings with a freecarve board.

Freecarving is not easy:

- You have to be good at snowboarding.

- You have to be very strong.

Snowboard competitions

There are lots of snowboarding competitions.

They are held all over the world

Competition	Where?
Half-pipe	Half-pipe
Boardercross	Race course with jumps and drops
Giant **slalom**	Race course with corners
Slope style	Slope
Big air	Very high jump

Cool Water
BIG AIR

What?	How do you win?
Take turns to do tricks	Best tricks
Race together	First to finish
Take turns to race	Best time
Take turns to do tricks	Best tricks
Take turns to do tricks	Best tricks

Quiz

1 What kind of sport is snowboarding?

2 Name the three kinds of snowboarding.

3 What kind of boots and bindings do freecarvers wear?

4 Where can you snowboard in the UK?

5 What does goofy mean?

6 Why are the edges of the board important?

7 What must you *not* do when you fall over?

8 What is powder snow?

9 Where do freestyle riders do their tricks?

10 When did snowboarding get into the Olympic Games?

Glossary of terms

avalanche	When lots of snow slides down a mountain very fast.
big air	A very good trick in the air.
board bag	A bag to keep a snowboard in.
board sport	A sport that you do on a board, e.g. surfboarding, skateboarding.
boardercross	A kind of racing that is like motocross on snowboards.
bunny slope	A slope that you start snowboarding on – it is not steep.
fakie	Riding with your front foot at the back and your back foot at the front when doing the trick 'fakie to forward'.
falling leaf	A way of going downhill on a snowboard.
glide	Moving along with both feet on the board.
goofy	Riding with the right foot in front.
regular	Riding with the left foot in front.
run	A race course.
shredders	People who are good at snowboarding.
skate	Moving along with one foot on the board.
ski resorts	Places that do winter sports holidays.
slalom	A downhill race course with very sharp corners.
snow cannon	A machine that makes snow.
twin-tips	Freestyle boards that are the same at both ends.
warm-up	Getting your body ready for exercise.

More resources

Books

Snowboarding, Radical Sports Series, Andy Fraser, Heinemann Library
(0-431-03678-0)

This book gives you tips on boards, kit and moves.

Snowboarding – The essential guide to equipment and techniques, Greg Goldman, Part of The Adventure Sports Series, New Holland, (1-85974-398-6)
This book has great photos and step-by-step pictures.

Magazines

Transworld Snowboarding, Trans World Media

Snowboarder Magazine, Primedia

There are lots of snowboarding magazines. These two magazines are full of news, tips and great photos.

Websites

http://www.abc-of-snowboarding.com
This website has everything you need. There are cartoons to show you how to do tricks.

http://www.snow-camp.co.uk
This website is about Snow-Camp – the winter sports charity. There is a great video about one of the trips.

DVDs and Videos

Extreme Snowboard (Cat. No. QLDVD6502)
This video shows the pros in action.

Wintermission (Cat. No. VHOT6697)
Great music and locations in the best British snowboarding movie ever!

Answers

1 A board sport

2 Freeride, freestyle, freecarve

3 Hard boots and bindings

4 Dry-ski slopes and snow centres

5 You put your right foot at the front of the board

6 They help you stop and turn

7 Put your hands in front of you

8 Snow that has just fallen

9 Snowboard parks

10 1998

Index